YOUR KNOWLEDGE HAS VALUE

Financial Analysis of the Airlines Qantas and Virgin Australia (2015 to 2017)

Vedhas Sabnis

G R I N ☺

Bibliographic information published by the German National Library:

The German National Library lists this publication in the National Bibliography; detailed bibliographic data are available on the Internet at http://dnb.dnb.de.

ISBN: 9783346288684
This book is also available as an ebook.

© GRIN Publishing GmbH
Nymphenburger Straße 86
80636 München

Print and binding: Books on Demand GmbH, Norderstedt, Germany
Printed on acid-free paper from responsible sources.

The present work has been carefully prepared. Nevertheless, authors and publishers do not incur liability for the correctness of information, notes, links and advice as well as any printing errors.

GRIN web shop: https://www.grin.com/document/948554

Emirates Aviation University

Financial Analysis for Managers

Financial Analysis of Qantas and Virgin Australia for (2015 to 2017)

Prepared by: Vedhas Sabnis

Table of Contents

List of Tables

1 Executive Summary

Qantas and Virgin Australia have been Australia's leading airlines and prime competitors in the regional market. An analyses of the airlines' financial performance in the period 2015, 2016 and 2017 is presented in this report.

The report begins with a short introduction into the dynamics of the airlines under review. A background knowledge of these carriers is important for studying the financial impact on them.

The basis of financial analysis is discussed thereafter where the 6 key financial analysis parameters (profitability, efficiency, liquidity, gearing, horizontal analysis and vertical analysis) are introduced, explained and summarized separately for each airline. Qantas fulfilled all criteria for a stable airline except in gearing and liquidity analysis whereas Virgin Australia fell short in profitability and efficiency.

A comparative analysis is provided where the performance of both Qantas and Virgin Australia is closely studied. A business performance review specific to Qantas is presented with focus on both financial and non financial aspects.

A conclusion is provided which details out the major findings which are a by-product of the analysis.

Lastly, few recommendations are provided based on the summarized conclusion which are of financial and non-financial nature.

Qantas was found to be highly profitable in this review period. Virgin Australia meanwhile suffered significant losses and was in recovery stage at the end of the analysis period.

2 Introduction

Air travel has evolved in leaps and bounds over the past few decades and a lot of its success is owed to periodic advancements in technology eventually making it the safest mode of transport available to us. However, unfortunate safety related incidents and accidents have occurred over the recent past and hence, safety has attained the highest priority among all airlines. In spite of all the concerns, Australian airlines have attained high safety ratings from AirineRatings.com which is a global ratings website. With more than 400 airlines under the website's radar, Australian airlines have outshone their global competitors to the effect that the country's 2 major carriers Qantas and Virgin Australia have attained rankings in the Top 20 safest airlines of 2018.

About Qantas

Qantas (the world's second oldest airline) was founded in Queensland in 1921 and has been in continuous operation since then, longer than any other airline. Qantas has particularly stood out among its competitors where experts have attributed its remarkable safety record, despite being 60 years old and hence rich in experience in countering challenges. They have a key and profitable partnership with Emirates which allows them to codeshare flights to Europe from Emirates' home base in Dubai.

About Virgin Australia

Virgin Australia, relatively nascent at 18 years old is proving to be a tough competitor, especially in the regional market with its relatively young fleet. Virgin Australia is a part of an alliance with Etihad Airways called Etihad Airways Partners. This alliance has helped them mimic the relation between Qantas and Emirates to a certain effect.

The dynamics of these Middle Eastern carriers also affect the Australian carriers by the virtue of their symbiotic relationship.

The following fact sheet provides a brief introduction to these airlines:

	Qantas	Virgin Australia
Year Established	1921	2000
Fleet Size	121	116
Destinations	85	52
Number of Employees	23000	9800

Table 1: Qantas and Virgin Australia brief introduction

This report aims to present a financial analysis of these airlines over the years 2015,2016 and 2017. The source for the figures is purely audited financial reports. The auditor for both these airlines is the Dutch firm KPMG. Both financial statements are presented as year ending 30th June for every year.

3 Financial Analysis

The four ratios, profitability, efficiency, liquidity and gearing offer the best approach for financial analysis of an entity. Coupled with horizontal and vertical analyses of the firms' balance sheets and income statements, the company's entire financial standing can be surmised.

All figures and values are taken from the audited reports of Qantas and Virgin Australia for the years 2015, 2016 and 2017 unless otherwise referenced.
(Virgin Australia audited annual report 2015), (Virgin Australia audited annual report 2016), (Virgin Australia audited annual report 2017) and (Qantas audited financial report 2015), (Qantas audited financial report 2016) (Qantas audited financial report 2017)

3.1: PROFITABILITY

Profitability of an entity, simply put, is the ability of that entity to earn profit. Profitability differs from profit as it is a measure of efficiency for success of the business. Whereas, a business is said to be in profit only if it pays all the expenses relating to the revenue generated by it.
Profitability can be determined with the help of profitability ratios. Common ratios used to analyze profitability are:

1. $Return\ on\ ordinary\ shareholder\ funds = \frac{Net\ Profit\ after\ taxation}{Share\ Capital + Reserves} x\ 100$

This ratio helps in determining the return on investment of shareholder funds. Mapping profit against share capital will be helpful for shareholders to invest in more shares or vice-versa.

2. $Return\ on\ capital\ employed = \frac{Net\ Profit\ after\ interest\ and\ taxation}{Share\ Capital + Reserves + Non-current\ liabilities} x\ 100$

This ratio is helpful in determining the return on all capital employed by the airline. This helps the airline in making cautious future decisions with investing additional capital with respect to their profit.

3. $Gross\ Profit\ Margin = \frac{Gross\ Profit}{Sales\ Revenue} x\ 100$

4. $Net\ Profit\ Margin = \frac{Net\ Profit\ before\ interest\ and\ taxation}{Sales\ Revenue} x\ 100$

Profit margin ratios are useful in determining the percentage profit gained with respect to the sales revenue after deduction of all expenses.

A sample calculation for the above ratios is provided in Annexure 1.

Analysis from Profitability results:

As per Qantas figures of 2015,2016 and 2017, the following was noted:

$M	Profitability			
Year	Return on Ordinary Shareholder funds	ROCE	Gross Profit Margin	Net Profit Margin
2015	12.27	5.01	6.63	6.63
2016	30.22	10.48	10.14	10.14
2017	26.08	8.65	8.53	8.53

Table 2: Profitability of Qantas

From the above table, it is clear that Qantas had dramatic returns on their ordinary shareholder funds over 2015 and 2016, however, there was a drop in their return in 2017. This drop in return is not to be deemed significant as is still more than 13% higher with respect to 2015.

A similar trend of great surge and then a drop can be observed in Return on capital employed (ROCE) for the years 2015,2016 and 2017.

As per the available figures, it was observed that Gross profit margin and the net profit margin were identical. There is minor deviation between the values of ROCE and the profit margins.

This common trend clearly showcases that Qantas has had a profitable outing in 2016 as compared to 2015 and 2017. Although the returns have been lower and thereby the profitability, Qantas still had a strong financial performance in 2017.

As per Virgin Australia figures of 2015,2016 and 2017, the following was noted:

$M	Profitability	
Year	Return on Ordinary Shareholder funds	ROCE
2015	-7.38	-2.52
2016	-15.76	-5.93
2017	-8.07	-3.92

Table 3: Profitability of Virgin Australia

From above, it can be seen that the company is facing significant losses. They had a very poor year in 2016 with respect to return on ordinary shareholder funds. Their return on capital employed was the lowest in the past 3 years in 2016. Due to the net loss, the profit margin calculations are irrelevant.

Summary:

New partnerships in 2016 such as the one with Airbnb had helped Qantas' consumers reach new avenues. Australia is a tourist heavy sector and Qantas' global reach has boosted the company's financials and profits manifold. Virgin Australia has also expanded locally, but it has not translated into profits for them. As seen from 2017, they are gradually moving towards profitability but it does not mask their poor financial performance in 2016 and 2017. Based only on its profitability, Qantas is definitely far ahead of its regional rival.

3.2: EFFICIENCY

Efficiency of an airline can be defined as the airline's ability to effectively face liabilities with judicious use of their resources and assets. (Efficiency ratio, Investopedia)

The efficiency ratios relevant to the airline industry are:

1. $Sales\ revenue\ to\ capital\ employed = \dfrac{Sales\ Revenue}{Share\ Capital + Reserves + Non-current\ liabilities} \times 100$

This ratio will be helpful in understanding whether the airline had managed to attain enough revenue with respects to all its investments and reserves.

2. $Sales\ revenue\ per\ employee = \dfrac{Sales\ revenue}{No.of\ employees}$

This ratio is helpful in understanding whether the no. of employees under the airline's payroll is justified with respect to the revenue. This is an important tool in regulating employee numbers and monitoring employee performance.

3. $Non\ Current\ Asset\ Turnover = \dfrac{Revenue}{Non-Current\ Asset}$

This ratio is helpful in determining how efficient the non-current assets have turned out as mapped against the revenue generated with respect to these assets. The decision to retire/acquire assets can be taken through this analysis.

A sample calculation for the above ratios is provided in Annexure 2.

Analysis from Efficiency results:

As per Qantas figures of 2015,2016 and 2017, the following was noted:

	Efficiency		
Year	Sales Revenue on Capital Employed	Sales Revenue per Employee	NCA turnover
2015	141.50	0.51	1.27
2016	164.94	0.51	1.22
2017	162.90	0.50	1.14

Table 4: Efficiency of Qantas

From the above table, it is observed that Qantas managed to significantly improve its revenue on capital employed in 2016 from 2015 and has also been somewhat consistent in 2017.
The number of employees on Qantas payroll in 2015, 2016 and 2017 are 31079, 31884 and 32268 respectively. (Qantas Data book 2015, Qantas Data book 2016 and Qantas Data book 2017)

A consistency can also be observed for sales revenue per employee throughout 2015, 2016 and 2017.
Non - current asset for Qantas largely is its fleet of aircraft. With the average life of an aircraft being 25 years, Qantas has managed to generate sufficient revenue with respect to its non –current asset.

s per Virgin Australia figures of 2015,2016 and 2017, the following was noted:

Year	Efficiency		
	Sales Revenue on Capital Employed	Sales Revenue per Employee	NCA turnover
2015	127.35	0.44	1.13
2016	132.54	0.53	1.16
2017	106.57	0.52	1.10

Table 5: Efficiency of Virgin Australia

om the above table, it can be seen that Virgin Australia managed to up its sales revenue on capital employed by most 5% in 2016 from 2015. However, it observed a significant drop of around 26% in 2017. This is attributed the increase in its non-current assets in 2017.

he number of employees on Virgin Australia Group payroll for the years 2015, 2016 and 2017 are 10800, 9500 d 9800 respectively.

les revenue per employee increased in 2016 as is evident from the reduction in the number of employees from)15 in 2016 (further the capital invested in 2016 was $272 million). In 2016 and 2017, the revenue per employee as consistent due to no major change in employee numbers and the revenue.

he non-current asset turnover has been largely consistent for the airline with no major overhauling of its fleet.

ummary:

he efficiency analysis gave a good insight into Qantas and Virgin Australia sales, capital and turnover over the 3 view years. As per the figures, it turned out that Qantas was more efficient than its rival Virgin Australia by rtue of sales revenue on capital employed but the 2 airlines were found to be equally efficient with respect to the venue per employee and NCA turnover mapping.

3.3: LIQUIDITY

Liquidity can be defined as the ability of a enterprise to adequately use its assets to manage existing liabilities. Liquidity can be determined by analyzing Current Ratio and Acid Test as:

1. $Acid\ test\ (or\ Quick\ ratio) = \dfrac{Current\ Asset\ (excluding\ inventories)}{Current\ Liabilities}$

This ratio is useful in determining balance between the current assets and liabilities of the airline. If the ratio is greater than 1, then the airline can be said to be financially very stable. However, in most cases the ratio seldom exceeds 1 as in the aviation business, these values are difficult to achieve.

A sample calculation for the above has been provided in Annexure 3.

Current ratio differs from Acid test as inventories are included as current assets in the Current ratio analysis. Since the industry in question does not include inventory, the current ratio is ignored.

Analysis from Liquidity results:

As per Qantas figures of 2015,2016 and 2017, the following was noted:

| Year | Qantas | | Liquidity |
	Current Asset (excluding inventories)	Current Liabilities	Acid Test
2015	4727	7642	0.62
2016	3122	7028	0.44
2017	2768	7095	0.39

Table 6: Liquidity of Qantas

As per the above figures, Qantas significantly reduced its assets throughout 2015, 2016 and 2017. This however did not reflect on their liabilities as the figure does not drastically change save from 2015. This further reduced their liquidity capability.

As per Virgin Australia figures of 2015,2016 and 2017, the following was noted:

| Year | Virgin Australia | | Liquidity |
	Current Asset (excluding inventories)	Current Liabilities	Acid Test
2015	1544.9	2299.8	0.67
2016	1671.4	2779.8	0.60
2017	1741.2	2348.3	0.74

Table 7: Liquidity of Virgin Australia

As per the above figures, the acid test result for Virgin Australia has had a consistently high acid test outcome which is evident from their low liability values across the 3 review years.

Summary:

From the liquidity analysis done for the 2 airlines, it was evident that Qantas' test outcome considerably worsened throughout the 3 years of review. In contrast Virgin Australia performed consistently with high acid test ratio. The airline's outcome was predominantly due to its low liability values.

3.4: GEARING

Gearing ratio analyses the company's long term debts with respect to the capital employed. (Gearing ratio, Investopedia)

Interest cover ratio is the measure of the profit before taxes and finance costs against the interest payable by the company.

Some tools to analyze gearing are:

1. $Gearing\ Ratio = \frac{Long\ term\ (Non\ Current)\ Liabilities}{Share\ Capital+Reserves+Non-current\ liabilities} x\ 100$

This ratio is useful in determining the extent of future loans an organization can avail. The higher the gearing ratio, the lower the airline's financial stability.

2. $Interest\ Cover\ Ratio = \frac{Profit\ Before\ Interest\ and\ Taxation}{Interest\ payable}$

This ratio is useful in determining the ease of the airline to pay its outstanding debt. An interest cover ratio of 2 is deemed acceptable for a solid, consistent revenue company.

A sample calculation for the above has been provided in Annexure 4.

Analysis from Gearing results:

As per Qantas figures of 2015,2016 and 2017, the following was noted:

Year	Gearing	
	Gearing Ratio	Interest Cover Ratio
2015	59.17	3.00
2016	65.33	5.79
2017	66.82	5.83

Table 8: Gearing of Qantas

As per the above figures, Qantas has an increasing gearing ratio trend observed throughout the review period. This implies that the airline is not sufficiently stable with respect to its financials.

As for the interest cover ratio, the trend observed has been a positive one for the airline. To have an interest cover ratio above 3 from 2015 onwards speaks of the generous revenue generated by the airline.

s per Virgin Australia figures of 2015,2016 and 2017, the following was noted:

Year	Gearing	
	Gearing Ratio	Interest Cover Ratio
2015	65.94	-0.53
2016	62.35	-11.56
2017	51.39	-5.14

Table 9: Gearing of Virgin Australia

s per the above figures, Virgin Australia has seen a decreasing trend of its gearing ratio as they have
anaged to limit their liabilities through the review period.

owever, their interest cover ratio has fallen into the negative domain due to them incurring a loss all
roughout the review period.

ummary:

s seen from the Gearing analysis of both Qantas and Virgin Australia, it can be concluded that Virgin
ustralia has inched ahead of Qantas as per the gearing ratio result. However, Qantas has shown a
markable result in the interest cover ratio analysis in which Virgin Australia has drastically fallen back.

3.5: HORIZONTAL ANALYSIS

Horizontal analysis is the perfect tool to study the relative changes in line items in a company over the given time period. There are 2 methods of output; Absolute and Percentage.

In the absolute method, the value of the line item is put forward which gives a direct view into the changes in financial status of the company over the review years. This method is generally preferred when the financials of a single company is analysed.

In the percentage method, the line items are presented as a percentage increase or decrease from the previous year. This method is employed when 2 different companies are to be analysed. This is beneficial when companies might differ in scale and size.

In this section, a horizontal analysis is performed on Qantas and Virgin Australia's balance sheets and income statements.

Balance Sheet

For the balance sheet horizontal analysis, the following is analysed:

1. Total non-current assets
2. Total current assets
3. Total non-current liabilities
4. Total current liabilities
5. Total Equity

Qantas:

The following was observed as per the horizontal analysis of Qantas Balance sheet:

Year	2017	2016		2015	
Analysis Factor	$ M	Change in financials (%)	$ M	Change in financials (%)	$ M
Total non-current assets	14102	6.5	13247	6.1	1248
Total current assets	3119	-9.8	3458	-31.5	504
Total non-current liabilities	6586	2.6	6417	-3.0	661
Total current liabilities	7095	1.0	7028	-5.9	747
Total Equity	3540	8.6	3260	-5.4	344

Table 10: Qantas Balance sheet Horizontal Analysis

13

1. Total Non current Assets: Over the review period, there is a steady rate of increment in Qantas' non current assets at 6%. This can also be seen from their NCA turnover which is consistent in 2015, 2016 and 2017.

2. Total Current Assets: A significant drop in Qantas current assets was seen in 2016 from 2015 where they diminished their current assets by 31%. This can be attributed to the high liabilities stacked up in 2015 which Qantas had to liquidate assets for. This can also be observed in the Liquidity analysis done previously. From 2016 to 2017, a further drop of 9.8% can be seen. This highly affected their Liquidity ratio in 2017 which was the lowest seen in the 3 years.

3. Total non-current liabilities: Qantas managed to diminish their liabilities in 2016 to 3% from 2015. Their strategy with respect to liquidating assets was key to this result. However, they further acquired liabilities of 2.6% more from their 2016 NCLs.

4. Total current liabilities: Qantas managed to further diminish their current liabilities by 5% in 2016 from 2015. This was also in conjunction to their strategy of liquidation of current assets, where they concentrated more on liquidating the assets to reduce their current liabilities. However, they gained 1% more in current liabilities in 2017. With high liability numbers, it can be safely assumed that this increment was not significant.

5. Total Equity: Qantas had faced diminished equity numbers in 2016 of 5.4% from 2015, however, they recovered well in 2017 with a significant increase in total equity of 8.6%.

Virgin Australia:

The following was observed as per the horizontal analysis of Virgin Australia Balance sheet:

Year	2017	2016		2015	
Analysis Factor	$ M	Change in financials (%)	$ M	Change in financials (%)	$ M
Total non-current assets	4568.3	5.6	4327.1	3.2	4193.6
Total current assets	1787.5	4.3	1713.7	8.1	1586
Total non-current liabilities	2433.7	3.0	2362.2	-3.9	2459
Total current liabilities	2348.3	-15.5	2779.8	20.9	2299.8
Total Equity	1573.8	75.1	898.8	-12.0	1020.8

Table 11: Virgin Australia Balance sheet Horizontal Analysis

1. Total Non current Assets: Over the review period, Virgin Australia's non current assets increased by 3.2% in 2016 and a further 5.6% in 2017. This can also be seen from their NCA turnover which is increased from 2015 in 2016. Acquiring these non current assets in 2017 however was not fruitful as the company suffered heavy losses in 2016 and 2017.

2. Total Current Assets: A significant increase in Virgin Australia's current assets was seen in 2016 from 2015 where they increased their current assets by 8.1%. From 2016 to 2017, a further increment of 4.3% can be seen. This strategy did not bode well for the carrier as they suffered losses in 2016 and 2017.

3. Total non-current liabilities: Virgin Australia managed to diminish their liabilities in 2016 to 3.9% from 2015. This reflected in their acid test result as they displayed good control in reducing liabilities. However, they further acquired liabilities of 3% more from their 2016 NCLs. However, their financial position stabilized to to best result on acid test in 2017.

4. Total current liabilities: Virgin Australia managed to significantly increase their current liabilities by 20.9% in 2016 from 2015. This can be concluded to be a major reason for their heavy losses in this year. They managed to reduce losses by decreasing their current liabilities in 2017 to 15.5 % of their current liabilities in 2017.

5. Total Equity: Virgin Australia had faced diminished equity numbers in 2016 of 12% from 2015, however, they recovered tremendously in 2017 with a significant increase in total equity of 75.1% of the previous year.

Income Statement

For the income statement horizontal analysis, the following is analysed:

1. Total Revenue

2. Total Expenditure on operations

3. Profit After Tax

4. Total comprehensive income

Qantas:

The following was observed as per the horizontal analysis of Qantas Income Statement:

Year	2017		2016		2015
Analysis Factor	$ M	Change in financials (%)	$ M	Change in financials (%)	$ M
Total Revenue	16057	-0.9	16200	2.4	15816
Total Expenditure on operations	14687	0.9	14557	-1.4	14768
Profit After Tax	853	-17.1	1029	83.8	560
Total Comprehensive Income	1033	21.5	850	52.3	558

Table 12: Qantas Income statement Horizontal Analysis

1. Total Revenue: Qantas total revenue increased in 2016 to 2.4% of the revenue in 2015. They subsequently faced a slight decrease of 0.9% in revenue in 2017. However, this value is very low to be considered a significant decrease.

2. Total Expenditure on operations: Qantas reduced their expenditure in 2016 by 1.4% of the previous year. Their expenditure however, slightly increased in 2017 by 0.9%. This constant expenditure can be attributed to the reduction in global fuel prices in 2016 and 2017.

3. Profit After Tax: 2016 was highly profitable for the airline with a significant increment of 83.8% from the previous year. They could not however replicate this success in 2017 as the profit dropped by 17 % from the previous year despite low operating costs.

4. Total comprehensive Income: Qantas retained a high sum in 2016 of about 52% from their previous amount. This is majorly attributed to the high profits generated in 2016. Qantas further managed to increase their retained income by 21% from 2016 in 2017 despite registering low profits. This could relate to high equity Qantas had managed to acquire in 2017.

Virgin Australia:

The following was observed as per the horizontal analysis of Virgin Australia Income Statement:

Year	2017		2016		2015
Analysis Factor	$ M	Change in financials (%)	$ M	Change in financials (%)	$ M
Total Revenue	5047.3	0.5	5021	5.7	4749.2
Total Expenditure on operations	5171.2	-2.0	5278.7	29.3	4082.7
Loss After Tax	185.8	-17.3	224.7	139.6	93.8
Total Comprehensive Loss	221.1	-8.2	240.8	-9.5	266

Table 13: Virgin Australia Income statement Horizontal Analysis

1. Total Revenue: Virgin Australia's total revenue increased in 2016 to 5.7% of the revenue in 2015. They subsequently faced a slight decrease of 0.5% in revenue in 2017. However, this value is very low to be considered a significant decrease.

2. Total Expenditure on operations: Virgin Australia increased their expenditure in 2016 by a whopping 29%% of the previous year. This was not a good outcome for them since they had faced significant losses in 2015. Their expenditure however, slightly decreased in 2017 by 2%. This poor record is the primary reason for their losses faced throughout 2015, 2016 and 2017.

3. Loss After Tax: 2016 was highly unprofitable for the airline with a very high loss percentage of 139.6% from the previous year. We have already attributed this loss to the

high expenditure rate in 2016. They, however managed to reduce their loss by 17.3%, which was still not enough for the airline to reach break even state.

4. Total comprehensive Loss: In 2016, Virgin Australia managed to control their total loss by 9.5% from the previous and further decreased their loss by 8.2% in 2017. This could relate to high equity Virgin Australia had managed to acquire in 2017. A good control over their liabilities also helped their case on their road to recovery.

Summary of Horizontal Analysis:

Horizontal analysis of Qantas and Virgin Australia provided a good method to analyze the changes in the airlines' financials throughout 2015, 2016 and 2017. The airlines' balance sheets and income statements were put under review and the airlines' entire financial performance was visible.

The major factors that came up were:

1. From review of Qantas balance sheet it was observed that they had diminished their current assets in 2016 by 31% from 2015 to make up for high amount of liabilities they had accumulated over the years. While this did not reflect in their profits, it affected their liquidity ratio significantly in 2016 and subsequently in 2017.

2. From review of Virgin Australia's balance sheet, it was observed that the total equity of the airline increased manifold in 2017 by almost 75% from 2016. This was a major reason in the company managing to cut their losses significantly in 2017.

3. From review of he Qantas income statement, it was observed that the company gained significant profits after tax deductions by almost 84% in 2016. This was a major contributor in reducing their liabilities in 2016. This also resulted in huge total comprehensive income numbers in 2016 and 2017.

4. From review of the Virgin Australia income statement, it was observed that the company suffered high losses in 2016 from which they could recover only marginally in 2017.

3.6: VERTICAL ANALYSIS

In the vertical analysis method, all line items in the financial statement are expressed as a percentage of a base amount determined by a base line item. In this section, Total Assets of the airlines are chosen as the base line item with respect to which the all percentages are derived. The analysis is done for the period 2015, 2016 and 2017. In the analysis done below, the comparison is done between items for the same year. In addition to total assets, the following line items are chosen:

1. Total current assets

2. Total non-current assets

3. Total current liabilities

4. Total non current liabilities

5. Total equity

Qantas:

The following was observed as per the vertical analysis of Qantas Balance sheet:

2017				2016				2015			
Total Assets ($M)	Analysis Factor	$ M	Percentage of Total Assets (%)	Total Assets ($M)	Analysis Factor	$ M	Percentage of Total Assets (%)	Total Assets ($M)	Analysis Factor	$ M	Percentage of Total Assets (%)
17221	Total non-current assets	14102	81.9	16705	Total non-current assets	13247	79.3	17530	Total non-current assets	12481	71.2
17221	Total current assets	3119	18.1	16705	Total current assets	3458	20.7	17530	Total current assets	5049	28.8
17221	Total non-current liabilities	6586	38.2	16705	Total non-current liabilities	6417	38.4	17530	Total non-current liabilities	6613	37.7
17221	Total current liabilities	7095	41.2	16705	Total current liabilities	7028	42.1	17530	Total current liabilities	7470	42.6
17221	Total equity	3540	20.6	16705	Total equity	3260	19.5	17530	Total equity	3447	19.7

Table 14: Qantas Balance sheet Vertical analysis

The Total Assets of Qantas were found to be $17,221 million, $16,705 million and $17,530 million in 2017, 2016 and 2015 respectively. All percentages have been measured from taking the total assets as base (or 100%).

1. Total Non - Current assets (NCAs): The total NCAs were found to be increasing in nature by Qantas by 71.2%, 79.3% and 81.9% in 2015, 2016 and 2017 respectively. It can be safely deduced that these NCAs formed the majority of their Total assets throughout the review period.

2. Total Current Assets(CAs): The CAs amounted to 28.8%, 20.7% and 18.1% in 2015, 2016 and 2017 respectively. Qantas has managed to reduce their current assets over the three years with these assets comprising of a share well short of a quarter of their Total Assets. This share further decreased in 2016 and 2017.

3. Total Non-current liabilities: Qantas' non current liabilities made up of about 37%, 38.4% and 38.2% of their total assets in 2015, 2016 and 2017 respectively. Their liabilities have not significantly changed in these years and hence no major change is observed in the review period.

4. Total Current Liabilities: Qantas' current liabilities are made up od about 42.6%, 42.1% and 41.2% of their total assets in 2015, 2016 and 2017 respectively. The constant liability argument can be repeated here and hence no major change observed.

5. Total Equity: Qantas' total equity as part of its assets has remained constant throughout the review period with minor fluctuation in 2016.

Virgin Australia:

The following was observed as per the vertical analysis of Virgin Australia Balance sheet:

2017				2016				2015			
Total Assets ($M)	Analysis Factor	$ M	Percentage of Total Assets (%)	Total Assets ($M)	Analysis Factor	$ M	Percentage of Total Assets (%)	Total Assets ($M)	Analysis Factor	$ M	Percentage of Total Assets (%)
6355.8	Total non-current assets	4568.30	71.9	6040.8	Total non-current assets	4327.10	71.6	5779.6	Total non-current assets	4193.60	72.6
6355.8	Total current assets	1787.5	28.1	6040.8	Total current assets	1713.70	28.4	5779.6	Total current assets	1586	27.4
6355.8	Total non-current liabilities	2433.7	38.3	6040.8	Total non-current liabilities	2362.2	39.1	5779.6	Total non-current liabilities	2459	42.5
6355.8	Total current liabilities	2348.3	36.9	6040.8	Total current liabilities	2779.8	46.0	5779.6	Total current liabilities	2299.8	39.8
6355.8	Total equity	1573.8	24.8	6040.8	Total equity	898.8	14.9	5779.6	Total equity	1020.8	17.7

Table 15: Virgin Australia Balance sheet Vertical analysis

The Total Assets of Virgin Australia were found to be $6,355.8 million, $6,040.8 million and $5779.6 million in 2017, 2016 and 2015 respectively. All percentages have been measured from taking the total assets as base (or 100%).

1. Total Non - Current assets (NCAs): The total NCAs were found to be fluctuating in nature by 72.6%, 71.6% and 71.9% in 2015, 2016 and 2017 respectively. It can be safely deduced that these NCAs formed the majority of their Total assets throughout the review period.

2. Total Current Assets(CAs): The CAs amounted to 27.4%, 28.4% and 28.1% in 2015, 2016 and 2017 respectively. Virgin Australia has managed to steady their current assets over the

three years with these assets comprising of a share marginally higher than a quarter of their Total Assets.

3. Total Non-current liabilities: Virgin Australia's non current liabilities made up of about 42.5%, 39% and 36.9% of their total assets in 2015, 2016 and 2017 respectively. Their liabilities have reduced in these years and hence a minor change is observed in the review period.

4. Total Current Liabilities: Virgin Australia's current liabilities are made up od about 39.8%, 46% and 36.9% of their total assets in 2015, 2016 and 2017 respectively.

5. Total Equity: Qantas' total equity as part of its assets has remained constant throughout the review period with minor fluctuation in 2016.

Summary of Vertical Analysis:

Vertical analysis of Qantas and Virgin Australia provided a good method to analyze the changes in the airlines' financials throughout 2015, 2016 and 2017 as a function of their total assets. The airlines' balance sheets were put under review and the airlines' entire financial performance was visible.

Two major points were observed:

A. From the review of Qantas balance sheet It was observed that Non current assets form a major share of their total assets as compared to Virgin Australia. However, this is justified by a larger fleet of Qantas and more destinations served by them.

B. From the review of Virgin Australia balance sheet, it was observed that when the airline reduced its total equity, it suffered major losses in 2016. However, with a significant increase in total equity in 2017, they were able to control their losses marginally.

3.7: Comparative analysis

The ratios analysed above are further consolidated in a table provided below. This table would be helpful in comparing Qantas and Virgin Australia's performance in the review period 2015,2016 and 2017.

Airline	Profitability				Efficiency			Liquidity	Gearing	
	Return on Ordinary Shareholder funds	ROCE	Gross Profit Margin	Net Profit Margin	Sales Revenue on Capital Employed	Sales Revenue per Employee	NCA turnover	Acid Test	Gearing Ratio	Interest Cover Ratio
Qantas	12.27	5.01	6.63	6.63	141.50	0.51	1.27	0.62	59.17	3.00
	30.22	10.48	10.14	10.14	164.94	0.51	1.22	0.44	65.33	5.79
	26.08	8.65	8.53	8.53	162.90	0.50	1.14	0.39	66.82	5.83
Virgin Australia	-7.38	-2.52	-1.48	-1.48	127.35	0.44	1.13	0.67	65.94	-0.53
	-15.76	-5.93	-5.12	-5.12	132.54	0.53	1.16	0.60	62.35	-11.56
	-8.07	-3.92	-2.41	-2.41	106.57	0.52	1.10	0.74	51.39	-5.14
Favourable financials	Qantas	Qantas	Qantas		Qantas	Virgin Australia	Qantas	Virgin Australia	Virgin Australia	Qantas

Table 16: Summary Table of Qantas and Virgin Australia for Comparative Analysis

From the above summary table, it is established that Qantas has had better financial impact over Virgin Australia within the review period. The profitability of Qantas has remained positive throughout and this is attributed to the fact that the airline has made huge profits in the three years. Qantas also has managed to to score high on the sales revenue on capital employed and non current asset turnover fronts. However, its financials dwindle when put to the acid test and also the gearing ratio. While a poor acid test does induce alarm over the state of its assets, the gearing ratio can be said to be acceptable for an airline. The airline makes up the gearing ratio results with the interest cover ratio where it is consistently improving. As per the horizontal analysis, Qantas had diminished their current assets to cover for their heavy liabilities in 2015. As per the vertical analysis, Qantas had majority of their total assets in the form of Non current assets.

It can be safely said that Virgin Australia has had a very poor year as is evident from the financial analysis shown above throughout the review period. The airline has suffered heavy loss throughout the 3 years, although it has made up significantly in the year 2017. The losses have also affected the airline's profitability index where the numbers are in the high negatives. As for the efficiency, the airline has managed to inch ahead of its rival Qantas in the sales revenue per employee test as the trend observed has been of the increasing kind from 2015 to 2016 and then consistent through 2017. The airline's best performance has been the acid test as it has managed to better control its assets and liabilities than Qantas. A decreasing trend of the gearing ratio which implies stable finances has worked in its favor. The losses have, however, affected its interest cover ratio which has again featured in the negative throughout the review period. As per the horizontal analysis, Virgin Australia managed to salvage their worst financial year in 2016 by increasing their total equity value considerably. As per the vertical analysis, Virgin Australia had a good control over their liabilities in 2016 and 2017.

4 Business Performance of Qantas (2015-2016-2017)

In section, the overall business performance of Qantas is covered from the review period 2015, 2016 and 2017.

Profits in all sectors, control over assets and liabilities and shareholder equity management are all good indicators of a successful enterprise. Qantas has managed to score highly in almost all sections. Surely, their liability numbers are very high but they have managed to control these with the help of liquidation of their assets.

Qantas is a true and true Australian airline as has been adequately reflected in its Australia centered business. This had helped them manage their business from their parent country effectively.

The airline has managed to earn good profits by virtue of their balanced scorecard and strict KPIs (key performance indicators). Some KPIs for their CEO include areas of strategy, customer, employees, relations with businesses and governments. The company also serves its employees well with a balanced scorecard approach to decide on employee remunerations. The STIP plan for executives and CEO is a measure of remuneration awarded for the work done. This is presented annually and is decided by a formula:

Value of STIP
= Base Pay x Target Opportunity x Scorecard result x Individual Performance factor

The airline's annual report forms a good example of responsibility report, wherein the Chairman, Director and the CEO comment on the economic standing of the company with respect to their own work done in that year. The Director's report consists of a section where the director answers company related questions posed specifically to him. This is a unique way to address concerns for the Board and transparency for employees and customers. The annual report is a one stop station for all employees, shareholders and customers to know about their company's financial standing in terms of full statement of profit and loss, balance sheet and revenue in that particular year. This report is duly audited by a reputable firm before it is released to the public.

5 Conclusion

The financial analysis conducted was useful in reviewing the financial positions of Australia's 2 leading carriers: Qantas and Virgin Australia. The review period for this analysis was from 2015-2017 using the financial indicators; profitability, efficiency, liquidity and financial gearing. Additionally, horizontal and vertical analysis were conducted on both airlines' income statement and balance sheets. All figures were taken from audited reports.

Major findings in all sectors are:

5. Profitability: Qantas turned out to be much profitable due to high profits earned during the review period. Virgin Australia however had poor returns in all 3 years. Their losses increased in 2016 and they could only marginally salvage losses in 2017. Based only on its profitability, Qantas is definitely far ahead of its regional rival.

6. Efficiency: Qantas was more efficient than its rival Virgin Australia by virtue of sales revenue on capital employed but the 2 airlines were found to be equally efficient with respect to the revenue per employee and NCA turnover mapping.

7. Liquidity: The primary attribute to unfavorable results for Qantas' liquidity ratio was the accumulation of high liabilities. However, Virgin Australia performed much better due to its low liabilities.

8. Gearing: Virgin Australia's long-term liabilities were significantly lower than Qantas, hence the lower gearing ratio. Due to losses, however, Virgin Australia could not generate a favorable interest cover ratio.

9. Horizontal and Vertical Analysis: From a deeper analysis of the income statement and balance sheet, it was observed that Qantas did not strive to control its liabilities in 2017 as they had done in 2016 despite high profits in 2016. As for Virgin Australia, they were prey to high operating costs all throughout the review period and hence suffered major losses in all 3 years.

Qantas has a significantly wider reach to the rest of the world in addition to a significant presence in the Australia-New Zealand region. Also, being a centralized business has worked in its favor.

Virgin Australia is a relatively newer airline, is competing with Qantas on almost all regional and international sectors has some catching up to do.

6 Recommendations

As an additional summary to the above conclusion, Qantas enjoyed profits across the 3 years of the review period, whereas Virgin Australia suffered losses throughout 2015, 2016 and 2017.

The following are recommended after due analysis of the financials of both airlines:

1. Looking at the profitability results, Virgin Australia should employ cost-cutting strategies to further control their losses. Virgin Australia has very low liabilities, and hence their assets could be utilized to counter losses. Liquidation of assets to cover losses and cost cuts would be beneficial for the airline to attain financial stability.

2. Low scores on the efficiency front (sales revenue on capital employed) by Virgin Australia also dented their chances at a profitable outcome. Their total expenditure on operations was also high in 2016 and 2017. Virgin Australia have to cut their operation costs to control their losses.

3. Qantas at the end of 2017 had amassed high liabilities. Their ideal strategy for a financially stable 2018 would be to invest their profits in reducing their high liabilities. If unforeseen circumstances arise, the company will have adequate liquidity and gearing ratio for survival.

4. Qantas would benefit immensely from a good marketing outlook. Their codeshare partner Emirates has a wider global reach and is popular throughout the world. One way to achieve this would be to invest in sports ventures. They already sponsor the Australian National cricket team and a further stake in another sporting club (e.g. football) would enable the company to extend its reach.

5. Virgin Australia is a codeshare member within the Etihad Airways Partners alliance. However, it does not enjoy the same privileges as Qantas does with Emirates. A push for benefits such as more route share from Australia and Abu Dhabi would be beneficial for the airline in the long run.

The above recommendations would be beneficial for the airlines to achieve financial stability in 2018 and beyond.

7 List of References

1. Investor.qantas.com. (2018).
   http://investor.qantas.com/FormBuilder/_Resource/_module/doLLG5ufYkCyEPjF1tpgyw/file/data-book/2015qantasdatabook.pdf [Accessed 25 Feb. 2018]

2. Investor.qantas.com. (2018).
   http://investor.qantas.com/FormBuilder/_Resource/_module/doLLG5ufYkCyEPjF1tpgyw/file/data-book/2016qantasdatabook.pdf [Accessed 25 Feb. 2018].

3. Investor.qantas.com. (2018).
   http://investor.qantas.com/FormBuilder/_Resource/_module/doLLG5ufYkCyEPjF1tpgyw/file/data-book/2017qantasdatabook.pdf [Accessed 25 Feb. 2018].

4. Staff, I. (2018). *Efficiency Ratio*. [online] Investopedia. Available at:
   https://www.investopedia.com/terms/e/efficiencyratio.asp [Accessed 1 Feb. 2018].

5. Staff, I. (2018). *Gearing*. [online] Investopedia. Available at:
   https://www.investopedia.com/terms/g/gearing.asp [Accessed 1 Feb. 2018].

6. Virginaustralia.com. (2018).
   https://www.virginaustralia.com/cs/groups/internetcontent/@wc/documents/webcontent/~edisp/annual-report-2015.pdf [Accessed 1 Feb. 2018]

7. Virginaustralia.com. (2018).
   https://www.virginaustralia.com/cs/groups/internetcontent/@wc/documents/webcontent/~edisp/2016-annual-report.pdf [Accessed 1 Feb. 2018].

8. Virginaustralia.com. (2018).
   https://www.virginaustralia.com/cs/groups/internetcontent/@wc/documents/webcontent/~edisp/2017-annual-report.pdf [Accessed 1 Feb. 2018].

8 Appendix – Sample Calculation Annexures

Annexure 1: Profitability

$$Return\ on\ ordinary\ shareholder\ funds = \frac{Net\ Profit\ after\ taxation}{Share\ Capital + Reserves} x\ 100$$

rom the Qantas figures for 2015,
et Profit After Taxation = $ 560,000,000
hare Capital = $4,630,000,000
eserves = ($66,000,000)
herefore, Return on Ordinary shareholder funds = (560000000/(4630000000-66000000))*100 = **12.27%**

$$Return\ on\ capital\ employed = \frac{Net\ Profit\ after\ interest\ and\ taxation}{Share\ Capital + Reserves + Non-current\ liabilities} x\ 100$$

rom the Qantas figures for 2015,
et Profit After Interest and Taxation = $ 560,000,000
hare Capital = $4,630,000,000
eserves = ($66,000,000)
on – current liabilities = $ 6,613,000,000
herefore, ROCE = (560000000/(4630000000-66000000+6613000000))*100 = **5.01%**

$$Gross\ Profit\ Margin = \frac{Gross\ Profit}{Sales\ Revenue} x\ 100$$

rom the Qantas figures for 2015,
ross Profit = $1,048,000,000
les Revenue = $15,816,000,000
herefore, Gross Profit Margin = 1048000000/15816000000*100 = **6.63%**

$$Net\ Profit\ Margin = \frac{Net\ Profit\ before\ interest\ and\ taxation}{Sales\ Revenue} x\ 100$$

rom the Qantas figures for 2015,
et Profit before Interest and Taxation = $1,048,000,000
les Revenue = $15,816,000,000
herefore, Net Profit Margin = 1048000000/15816000000*100 = **6.63%**

Annexure 2: Efficiency

1. $Sales\ revenue\ to\ capital\ employed = \frac{Sales\ Revenue}{Share\ Capital+Reserves+Non-current\ liabilities} x\ 100$

From the Qantas figures for 2015,
Sales Revenue = $ 158,160,000,000
Share Capital = $4,630,000,000
Reserves = ($66,000,000)
Non – current liabilities = $ 6,613,000,000
Therefore, Sales revenue to capital employed = (158160000000/ (4630000000-66000000+6613000000)) *100 = **141.50%**

2. $Sales\ revenue\ per\ employee = \frac{Sales\ revenue}{No.of\ employees}$

From the Qantas figures for 2015,
Sales Revenue = $ 158,160,000,000
Number of Employees = 31079
Therefore, Sales revenue per employee = **0.51**

3. $Non\ Current\ Asset\ Turnover = \frac{Revenue}{Non-\ Current\ Asset}$

From the Qantas figures for 2015,
Revenue = $ 158,160,000,000
Non-current assets = 12481
Therefore, non current asset turnover = **1.27**

27

Annexure 3: Liquidity

$$Acid\ test\ (or\ Quick\ ratio) = \frac{Current\ Asset\ (\ excluding\ inventories)}{Current\ Liabilities}$$

From the Qantas figures for 2015,
Current Asset (excluding inventories) = $4,729,000,000
Current Liabilities = $7,642,000,000

Therefore, Acid Test or quick ratio = 4729000000/7642000000 = **0.62**

Annexure 4: Gearing

$$.\ Gearing\ Ratio = \frac{Long\ term\ (Non\ Current)\ Liabilities}{Share\ Capital + Reserves + Non-current\ liabilities} x\ 100$$

From the Qantas figures for 2015,
Long term non - Current Liabilities = $6,613,000,000
Share Capital = $4,630,000,000
Reserves = ($66,000,000)
Non – current liabilities = $ 6,613,000,000

Therefore, gearing ratio = 6613000000/(4630000000-66000000-6613000000)*100 = **59.17%**

$$.\ Interest\ Cover\ Ratio = \frac{Profit\ Before\ Interest\ and\ Taxation}{Interest\ payable}$$

From the Qantas figures for 2015,
Profit before Interest and Taxation = $1,048,000,000
Interest Payable = $349,000,000

Therefore, gearing ratio = 1048000000/349000000= **3**

YOUR KNOWLEDGE HAS VALUE